Skateboarding

by Julie Murray

Abdo Kids Jumbo is an Imprint of Abdo Kids
abdobooks.com

abdobooks.com

Published by Abdo Kids, a division of ABDO, P.O. Box 398166, Minneapolis, Minnesota 55439.

Printed in the United States of America, North Mankato, Minnesota.

102022

012023

Photo Credits: Alamy, Getty Images, Shutterstock

Production Contributors: Teddy Borth, Jennie Forsberg, Grace Hansen
Design Contributors: Candice Keimig, Pakou Moua

Library of Congress Control Number: 2022937179

Publisher's Cataloging-in-Publication Data

Names: Murray, Julie, author.

Title: Skateboarding / by Julie Murray

Description: Minneapolis, Minnesota : Abdo Kids, 2023 | Series: Artistic sports | Includes online resources and index.

Identifiers: ISBN 9781098264246 (lib. bdg.) | ISBN 9781098264802 (ebook) | ISBN 9781098265083 (Read-to-Me ebook)

Subjects: LCSH: Skateboarding--Juvenile literature. | Action sports (Extreme sports)--Juvenile literature. | Skateboards--Juvenile literature. | Sports--Juvenile literature. | Sports--History--Juvenile literature.

Classification: DDC 796.22--dc23

Table of Contents

Skateboarding

Skateboarding is a popular sport! It involves riding on a skateboard. Skaters perform tricks and jumps on their skateboards.

The first skateboards were created in the 1940s. Wheels were **mounted** on the bottom of wooden boards and boxes.

The first **commercial** skateboard came out in 1959. The sport gained popularity throughout the world in the 1970s.

Los Angeles, USA
1978
China
1978
United Kingdom
1977

Today, skateboarding is both a **recreational** and **competitive** sport. Skaters go head-to-head in many competitions, like ESPN's X Games. Skateboarding is also a Summer Olympic event!

JPN

Types of Skateboarding

There are many kinds of skateboarding. Street skating is done in public areas. Riders do jumps and tricks on sidewalks and staircases. Many cities offer public skate parks.

NIKE
SB

Vert skating is done on vertical ramps, like a half-pipe. Big air is done off a mega ramp. Skaters use the ramps to gain speed to perform tricks.

THE REAL COST
GAMES
GAMES
SHREDHATE

Tricks

The ollie and the kickflip are basic tricks. Tony Hawk landed a 900 in the 1999 X Games. At the 2021 X Games, 12-year-old Gui Khury landed a 1080. That is three full rotations before landing!

ENERGY DRINK

Equipment

Skateboards have three parts. These are the **deck**, **trucks**, and wheels. Short boards are used for tricks. Longboards are used for cruising.

truck
wheel
deck
BIRD HOUSE

Skateboarding can be dangerous. Riders should wear safety equipment. Helmets, wrist guards, and knee and elbow pads are a must!

More Facts

- Skateboarding used to be called "sidewalk surfing." Surfers rode skateboards when there were no waves to ride.
- The first skate park opened in Jacksonville, Florida, in 1976.
- Skateboarding is a newer sport at the Summer Olympics. It first appeared at the 2020 Games in Tokyo, Japan.

Glossary

commercial – having to do with making money.

competitive – a situation in which people are trying to win.

deck – or skate deck, the flat board you stand on when skateboarding.

mounted – attached or set in place.

recreational – an activity that is done for fun.

trucks – the steering devices on the bottom of the board.

Index

Visit **abdokids.com** to access crafts, games, videos, and more!

Use Abdo Kids code

ASK4246

or scan this QR code!